FAMOUS ARTISTS

LEONARDO
DA VINCI

ANTONY MASON

A WATTS BOOK
LONDON • NEW YORK • SYDNEY

CONTENTS

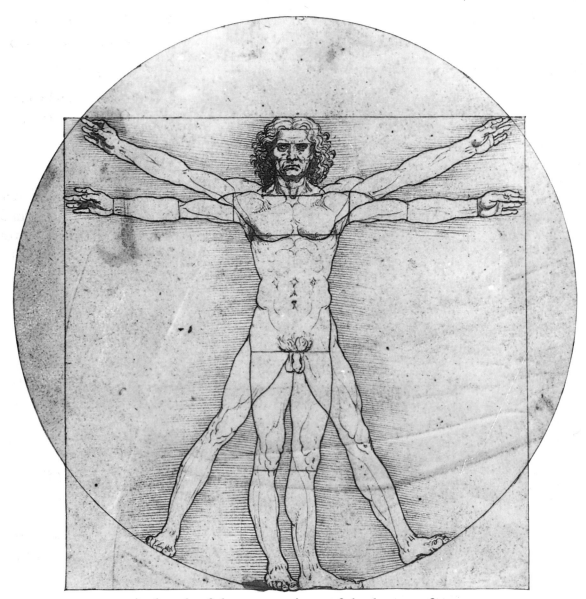

A sketch of the proportions of the human figure

INTRODUCTION

Leonardo da Vinci (1452-1519) was famous even in his own lifetime as a man of great brilliance, and one of Italy's most gifted painters. From an early age he was driven by a restless energy. He struggled to make his painting and drawing perfect. He also made detailed studies of nature, of the anatomy of the human body, and of mechanics – the workings of machines and the forces that make things move. By applying his imagination to these studies, he came up with some remarkable ideas. Sketches from his notebooks have turned out to resemble tanks, aeroplanes, helicopters and many other machines that were invented up to 400 years after his death.

This book explores Leonardo's development from apprentice to great artist. It traces the story of Leonardo's life, and explains how his major works came to be created. The artist's techniques are discussed and you can try some out. Below you can see how the book is organised.

An englargement of
part of the painting

The story of
the artist's life

Illustration of
the artist's home
or environment

About the
artist's
work at
the time

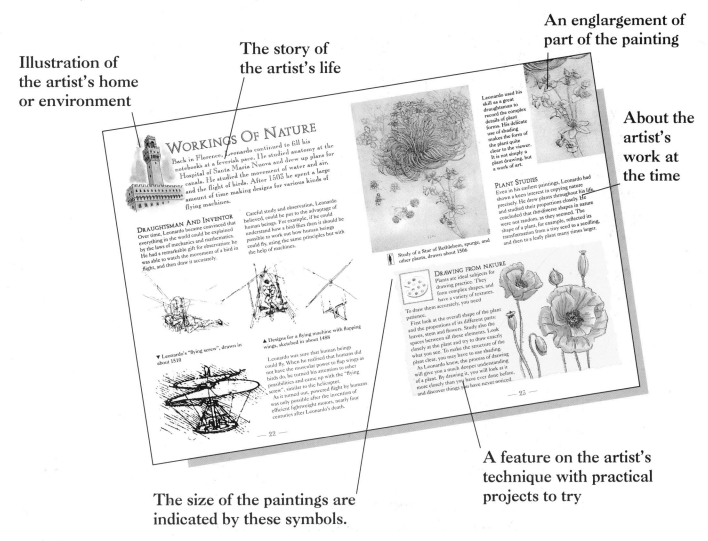

A feature on the artist's
technique with practical
projects to try

The size of the paintings are
indicated by these symbols.

LEARNING THE TRADE

Leonardo da Vinci was born during an exciting period of Italian history, later known as the Renaissance. In the 1300s, a love of Greek and Roman culture led to a revival in learning and the arts. The wealthy city-states of Italy, such as Florence, near Leonardo's birth-place, now attracted some of the most brilliant scholars, artists, and craftsmen of the times.

Vinci in central Italy

THE BOY FROM VINCI

In April 1452 a peasant girl called Caterina gave birth to a baby boy called Leonardo in a village near the small town of Vinci. The father was Ser Piero, who was not married to Caterina. He was a wealthy lawyer and landowner, much respected in Florence, which lay 25 kilometres to the east. Caterina later married a local man, and from the age of five Leonardo lived at Ser Piero's house.

APPRENTICESHIP

The young Leonardo received a standard education for the time, but already he showed a great talent for painting. It is said that Ser Piero first became aware of his son's gifts when Leonardo decorated a shield with a painting of a dragon. Based on drawings of

frogs and lizards, the painting was so realistic that it gave his father a fright.

When he was about 15 years old, Leonardo was sent to train as a painter and sculptor in the studio of one of the great artists of Florence, Andrea del Verrocchio (1435-88). Along with other young apprentices, Leonardo was taught the skills of drawing, painting and sculpture. He also helped with some of Verrocchio's own paintings.

The angel from Verrocchio's *Baptism of Christ*, painted by Leonardo in about 1472

The Annunciation was painted in about 1473, when Leonardo was in his early 20s.

The Annunciation portrays the scene from the New Testament when the Virgin Mary is told by the Angel Gabriel that she will give birth to Jesus. Leonardo used oil paint and tempera (powdered colour mixed with egg yolk) on a wooden panel.

The design of the painting is rather stiff and formal, but it shows Leonardo's careful attention to detail. The lily held by the angel, for example, is clearly drawn from nature. Many flowers had symbolic meanings in Leonardo's day. The lily was a symbol of the Virgin Mary.

PERSPECTIVE

By the early 15th century artists had discovered "linear" perspective – how distance could be represented on a flat picture. They realised that objects look smaller the further away they are. The edges of regular shapes such as walls follow angled lines which meet in the distance at "vanishing point". Try a perspective drawing yourself. Study how angled lines recede into the distance, and copy this. Pencil lines like those here may help.

THE PROFESSIONAL ARTIST

After Leonardo had completed his training at Verrocchio's studio he became a professional artist. He appears to have had no shortage of work. However, he was already showing a failing from which he suffered all his life: gifted though he was, he often lost interest in large projects and abandoned them before they were completed.

A MODEL PUPIL

Leonardo was one of the stars of Verrocchio's studio. It is said that the master was so impressed by Leonardo's work that he gave up painting and concentrated on sculpture.

Leonardo could not have hoped for a better training. It was hard work: he had to study drawing, and learn all the techniques of mixing colours, painting, and sculpting in stone and bronze. He also studied the mechanics of gears and levers, geometry and anatomy. After six years, his apprenticeship was complete. In 1472 he became a member of the Guild of St Luke. Many professions were organised into guilds. These protected the interests of members, and made sure that standards were maintained.

A STUDIO OF HIS OWN

Leonardo soon had a studio of his own in Florence. In his 20s he was a good-looking man, with long, flowing fair hair and bright blue eyes. He paid great attention to his appearance. He loved animals and was good at riding horses. He was also a vegetarian, which was unusual in his day. He was popular, known for his jokes, and a gifted musician. But he was also a rather solitary person, and devoted all his energies to his work. He never married.

The Adoration of the Magi, an unfinished painting begun in about 1481

This picture depicts the New Testament scene when the three kings present their gifts to the baby Jesus. Leonardo's brown underpainting shows that he aimed to portray the whole range of human emotions that might be felt by those present at such an important historical moment.

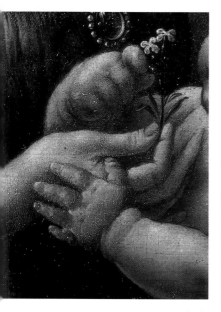

Leonardo painted a number of pictures of the Virgin Mary with Jesus. The hands and flower in *The Benois Madonna* show careful observation of detail. Here too the flower is symbolic: known as *Cruciferae*, it represents the cross (crucifix) on which Jesus would die as a man.

LIGHT AND SHADOW

Leonardo showed a great talent in making the human body look rounded and solid. He managed this by showing how light and shadow fall on faces, limbs and clothes. He saw the advantage of using oil paints to achieve this, as they allow the artist to build up layers of colour in rich tones. Oil painting had been developed in the Netherlands and was still a new technique in Italy.

The Benois Madonna was painted in about 1480.

PAYING FOR ART

For hundreds of years the Christian Church had been the main patron (supporter) of the arts. The Church had become very wealthy through donations and contributions. The best paintings, sculpture and architecture were done for churches and abbeys and for the palaces of powerful clergy. This is why many paintings had religious subjects. During the Renaissance wealthy rulers and merchants also became important patrons. As well as religious works, they commissioned portraits and even scenes from Greek and Roman mythology.

Pope Sixtus IV by Melozzo da Forli

New Horizons

Leonardo had just begun to establish his reputation as a painter in Florence when, in 1482, he decided to go to work in Milan. This great city in northern Italy was ruled by a new, young duke called Ludovico Sforza, who gave Leonardo the opportunity to use more of his many talents – for here he was to work not just as a painter, but also as an architect and engineer.

A Varied Job

Milan did not have the same reputation as Florence for painting and the arts. So it was quite a triumph for Ludovico Sforza to entice such a celebrated young artist as Leonardo away from Florence.

Leonardo's title was "Painter and Engineer to the Duke". His job involved a wide range of duties: painting portraits, designing sets and costumes for court festivals and shows, working on sculptures for the city, and giving advice on military architecture and city defences, and on mechanical engineering.

A portrait of Ginevra de Benci, painted either about 1474, or in 1481

A study for the angel's head in *Virgin of the Rocks*, drawn in about 1483

Leonardo appreciated his new role, and the freedom it gave him to pursue his many interests. He stayed in Milan for 17 years. By this time his skills as a painter were at their peak. The portrait of Ginevra de Benci shows many features that Leonardo would repeat for the rest of his life. He completed only about 25 paintings during his life, and of these only about 10 have survived.

This picture portrays a scene from the life of Jesus. It shows Jesus as a baby, with Mary and an angel (right), blessing the child who was to grow up to be St John the Baptist. Leonardo painted another version between 1494 and 1508.

The Virgin of the Rocks, painted in 1483-85

THE VIRGIN OF THE ROCKS

This painting shows Leonardo at the height of his powers as a painter. The figures are beautifully *modelled* – painted so that they look round and solid. Their expressions are calm, dignified and gentle. A rocky landscape is the setting for a meeting which is recorded in myth, not in the New Testament itself. The plants in the foreground are painted with great precision, while the distant landscape fades away in a blue haze. This effect is known as *sfumato*, which means "hazy" or "smoky" in Italian. The result is a mixture of rich and intense foreground, and dreamy distance. This near-and-far effect was a favourite technique of Leonardo, one he had tried out earlier in the portrait of Ginevra de Benci.

COMPOSITION

Leonardo had a scientific approach to composition – how the elements of a painting are arranged. He used simple shapes such as triangles and circles. In *The Virgin of the Rocks* a triangle joins Mary, St John and Jesus. A secondary shape, a circle, includes the angel. Base a composition of your own on simple shapes. Try the elements you want to include in different positions until you are happy with the result.

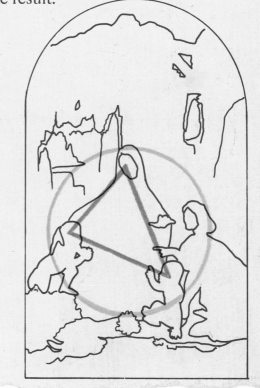

COURT PAINTER

As court painter, part of Leonardo's job was to portray people from the court of Ludovico Sforza in Milan (shown left). Most of his portraits are of women, wives of rich and famous noblemen. They look young, beautiful and serene. These portraits may be partly idealised, but Leonardo also managed to capture the characters of his different subjects.

TRUE PORTAITS

In Milan Leonardo developed more theories about painting. He believed that careful observation led to understanding, and that artists had an important role to play because they could record this understanding in precise and accurate images. He made many sketches of everything around him, particularly faces and parts of the body. He also observed the way that light fell on faces, fingers, hair and clothes, revealing their structure. He applied what he had learnt to his portraits. His use of light and shadow made the figures look solid and lifelike. The effect is called *chiarosuro*, which means "light-dark" in Italian.

In his portraits Leonardo took great trouble over the details, such as jewellery, cloth and hair. This can be seen here in the strands of curly hair. For some reason this painting was never finished: the clothes have been only roughly sketched in.

Another artist using such a delicate, smooth technique might have made the sitter look simply pretty and rather characterless. But in his portraits Leonardo aimed to show not just what the sitters looked like, but their mental state as well – the sort of people they were.

 Portrait of a Musician, painted in about 1485

Cecilia Gallerani was Ludovico Sforza's mistress. The ermine was included as a witty kind of joke: the Greek word for ermine is similar to her name. As we might expect, Leonardo painted the ermine with great care and precision.

MASTER OF PORTRAITURE

What distinguished Leonardo's painting was his ability to make everything look solid and three-dimensional. He managed this through close examination of shadow, and careful use of colour. In this, Leonardo was at least 50 years ahead of his time. Other painters were struggling with the same problem, but most of their work looks flat compared to his. Leonardo gives additional force to his portraits by using plain, dark backgrounds. These make the effect of light falling on the smooth skin of his sitters even more striking.

Portrait of Cecilia Gallerani, painted between 1495 and 1486

LIGHT AND DARK

If you look at any three-dimensional object, you can see that light falls on its surfaces in different ways. Surfaces facing the light are the brightest, while those facing away from the light are in shade. On curved surfaces the shadow gradually becomes darker as it curves away from the light. Try a study of this yourself, with a group of simply-shaped objects like those shown here. Shadow can be shown by shading, or by using darker colour.

NOTEBOOK STUDIES

During his 17 years in Milan, Leonardo produced countless drawings, of architecture, plants, people, anatomy, mechanics, mathematics – in fact, of just about everything he found interesting. Some of these are hasty sketches, others are very detailed illustrations. Some 7000 pages of illustrated notes have survived, but many thousands of pages have been lost.

TIRELESS QUESTIONING

Leonardo believed that knowledge should be based on observation. He formed a grand plan: to record the structure of everything in the world, in the belief that this would reveal laws of harmony and proportion that were thought to underlie all things. This was a hopeless task, and remained unfinished.

A study of grotesque heads, perhaps for a play, drawn between 1485 and 1490

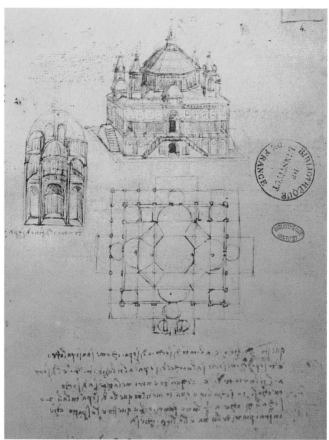

An architectural study, showing the plan of a church

Leonardo was a true "Renaissance man", gifted with many talents and ceaselessly questioning. He had not been educated at university, and approached learning in an original but very thorough manner. For example, he studied anatomy by dissecting dead bodies at a hospital. This was common practice for doctors, but not for artists.

Backward writing

Leonardo was left-handed. In the days of writing with pen and ink this was a disadvantage: as you pushed the pen forward your hand would trail over the fresh ink. Leonardo had a better idea. He wrote back to front, from right to left. His writing is "mirror writing": it is like ordinary writing held up to a mirror.

You can read mirror writing by using a mirror. But in fact it is quite easy to read it without a mirror, once you get used to it. It is also not that difficult to write. If you are right-handed, try writing backwards with your left hand. If you are left-handed, try using your right hand. You could start by writing your name in mirror writing.

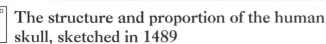

The **structure and proportion of the human skull**, sketched in 1489

OBSERVE AND INVENT

Leonardo was not simply a skilled draughtsman (someone who can draw). He studied people and objects closely, and made detailed sketches. But he could also apply his imagination to create something new – monsters or fairytale characters (shown on opposite page).

Try doing the same. Start by drawing a face as accurately as you can in pencil. Now rub out some of the features and exaggerate them in some way – for instance, give the face pointed elf-like ears, or an extra-long nose. You will see how easy it is to turn pictures of the real world into images from dreams and myth.

THE FRUITS OF WAR

In Milan Leonardo had to devote a certain amount of his time and energy to public monuments and to military engineering. He applied his original mind to both these duties. These were troubled times. The Italian city-states were constantly at war with each other, and they were also caught up in a war between France and Spain.

DESIGNING WEAPONS

Gunpowder had been introduced to Europe in the 14th century, and Leonardo knew that this would affect the development of warfare. He made designs for many weapons: multi-barrelled guns, a mechanism for firing hand-held guns, streamlined missiles with tail fins, and fortresses which could make the best use of cannons. He also worked on a variety of non-military machinery, such as cranes, cutting tools, mechanical looms and wire-making equipment.

GLORIES OF WAR

Leonardo's only major work of sculpture was a huge statue, 6.7 metres (22 feet) tall, of Francesco Sforza, Ludovico's father, mounted on a horse. He worked on this project on and off for 12 years, and completed a full-sized clay model for it in 1493.

Design for a chariot with revolving blades, and for a wooden armoured car, 1487

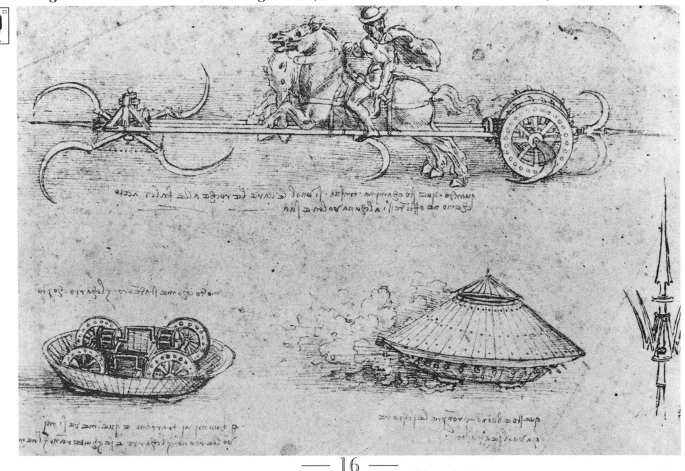

STATUE OF FRANCESCO SFORZA

Leonardo aimed to cast his equestrian, or mounted, statue of Francesco Sforza in bronze, but its huge size posed difficulties. His studies for the statue demonstrate his great skill in animal drawing. The sculpture was designed to portray the controlled power of the horse, and the mastery of its rider. In the first version the weight of the horse was to be cleverly supported by the figure of a fallen warrior. But it was impossible to cast this, so in the second version the horse was simply walking. It became the model for many equestrian statues made by other sculptors in later times.

The statue was so vast that it needed enormous quantities of bronze to make it. The bronze was in fact collected and ready to use. But Milan came under threat of attack by the French, and the bronze was used to make cannons. Despite his best efforts, and ingenious ideas for bronze casting, the statue was never completed.

A sketch for the equestrian statue of Francesco Sforza, 1488

Studies of horses, for the Sforza monument, drawn in 1490

MAKING A CAST

Bronze casting is an ancient way of making statues. First a model of the statue is made, usually of clay or wax. This is covered with an outer layer of clay, so that the shape of the model is imprinted into it. This outer layer is the mould. The model is removed, then molten bronze is poured into the

mould, filling the shape of the statue.

You can try the same idea by pressing an object such as a shell into modelling clay. Carefully peel the shell away from your clay mould. Now mix up a little plaster of Paris and pour it into the mould, filling the shape made by the shell. Allow it to dry overnight, then remove the mould to reveal the cast image of your shell.

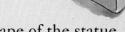

THE LAST SUPPER

In 1495 Leonardo began work on his largest and most ambitious painting. "The Last Supper" was painted on the wall of the monks' refectory (dining room) at the Convent of Santa Maria delle Grazie in Milan, shown on the left. Unfortunately Leonardo could not resist carrying out an experiment at the same time, and it went dramatically wrong.

A Technical Disaster

Leonardo spent just over two years on *The Last Supper*. He spent long periods of time sitting and contemplating his work, much to the frustration of his patrons, who thought he was wasting time. Because he wanted to be able to work slowly, and wanted his painting to have strong, rich colours, he decided not to use the fresco technique, but to try tempera (ground colour mixed with egg yolk) on a dry plaster base. Unfortunately the painting started to fall to pieces within 20 years, and was ruined by 1560s. What we see today is a pale, shadowy version of the original, frequently restored. It is still enough to show us the great power and mastery of this work.

The Last Supper was painted between 1495 and 1498.

The New Testament story of the Last Supper tells how Christ made a dramatic announcement during the meal with his apostles, foretelling that one of them would betray him. Leonardo portrays the apostle who would do so, Judas, leaning back with his face in shadow.

Giotto (1266-1337) painted this fresco using the traditional technique.

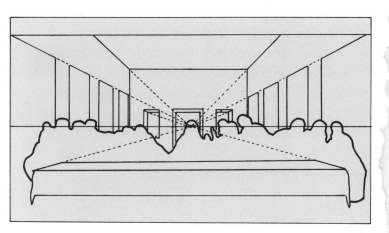

The Last Supper was one of Italy's most celebrated paintings during Leonard's own lifetime. Its subject was most suitable for a monks' dining room. As they ate, the monks could gaze up and contemplate this sacred meal. Leonardo designed the picture so that the scene forms part of the dining hall. He threatened to base the image of Judas on the prior of the convent, because the prior was so impatient with the artist's progress.

The vanishing point for the perspective is Christ's right eye, making Christ the central focus of the picture. His head is framed by the window overlooking a distant landscape. Christ is set apart from the two groups of figures to either side of him, and he is the only one who remains calm amidst the agitation of the apostles.

FRESCO PAINTING

Many of the great paintings of the Renaissance were wall-paintings, created to decorate churches and palaces. Most were frescos. *Fresco* means fresh: the artist applied the paint quickly to freshly laid, wet plaster. The result was a hard, long-lasting surface. The disadvantage of fresco painting was that it had to be applied in small patches, before the plaster dried. The artist had little opportunity to alter the painting once the plaster was dry.

THE MONA LISA

In 1499 France attacked Milan and Ludovico Sforza was forced to flee. In 1500, at nearly 50 years of age, Leonardo left Milan and travelled first to Mantua, then to Venice. Then he returned to Florence, where he was welcomed as one of the greatest artists of his time. He was about to begin one of the most fruitful periods of his life.

BACK IN FLORENCE

The capture of Milan by the French must have been a depressing experience for Leonardo. His 17-year appointment came to an end, and he lost his great patron, Ludovico Sforza. He also lost his statue: the clay model of his magnificent monument to Francesco Sforza was used by French soldiers as a target for shooting practice.

He had plenty of admirers, however. At her palace in Mantua (above) he drew a portrait of his hostess, Isabella d'Este, who requested a painted portrait from him in vain. In Venice he advised the Signoria (the city's governing council) on military defence. He made inventive sketches for underwater diving gear and webbed "watershoes" which looked like modern diving fins.

Back in Florence he stayed as a guest of an order of monks. He worked on various religious paintings and continued his studies of mathematics. In about 1503 he was asked by a wealthy Florentine called Francesco del Giocondo to paint a picture of his 26-year-old wife, Mona Lisa. This portrait is now one of the most famous paintings in the world.

Leonardo's portrait of Isabella d'Este appears to be a "cartoon" – a full-sized sketch which would be used to plot out a final painting. It is the only surviving work by Leonardo in pastel. The hand, the pose and the expression are all very similar to those used in *The Mona Lisa*.

 The portrait of Isabella d'Este, drawn in pastel in 1500

A Famous Smile

The Mona Lisa was one of Leonardo's favourite paintings, and it remained with him until he died. The smooth, rounded features are similar to some of Leonardo's other portraits of women, and to his paintings of the Virgin Mary. The woman in this portrait has an expression of great dignity and calm. Her mouth hovers at the edge of a smile, giving her a sense of mystery. This is the most celebrated smile in the history of painting.

Leonardo had studied the shape and structure of hands closely, so could paint them with confidence. They form a vital part of the composition of this portrait. Cover them over, and see how the balance of the painting alters.

Leonardo became famous for his background *sfumato* landscapes, which repeated the near-and-far effect seen even in his earliest portraits. Here the fanciful, rocky landscape occupies the entire background, dropping away to the hazy blue distance.

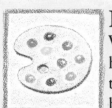 *The Mona Lisa*, also known as *La Gioconda*, painted in about 1503

Painting A Portrait

When Leonardo studied anatomy, he took precise measurements of the head. The proportions of the head are shown on the right. It is useful to follow them when you are working from imagination or drawing from life. The face is oval, and the eyes and nose line up on it in the form of a cross. The bottom of the mouth is about half-way between the base of the nose and the chin. Lightly sketch in lines for the features before you draw the face in detail.

WORKINGS OF NATURE

Back in Florence, Leonardo continued to fill his notebooks at a feverish pace. He studied anatomy at the Hospital of Santa Maria Nuova and drew up plans for canals. He studied the movement of water and air, and the flight of birds. After 1503 he spent a large amount of time making designs for various kinds of flying machines.

DRAUGHTSMAN AND INVENTOR

Over time, Leonardo became convinced that everything in the world could be explained by the laws of mechanics and mathematics. He had a remarkable gift for observation: he was able to watch the movement of a bird in flight, and then draw it accurately.

Careful study and observation, Leonardo believed, could be put to the advantage of human beings. For example, if he could understand how a bird flies then it should be possible to work out how human beings could fly, using the same principles but with the help of machines.

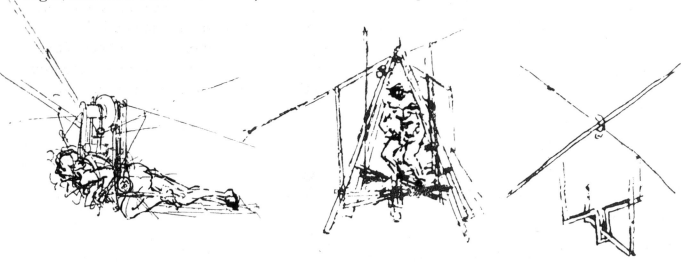

▼ Leonardo's "flying screw", drawn in about 1510

▲ Designs for a flying machine with flapping wings, sketched in about 1488

Leonardo was sure that human beings could fly. When he realised that humans did not have the muscular power to flap wings as birds do, he turned his attention to other possibilities and came up with the "flying screw", similar to the helicopter.

As it turned out, powered flight by humans was only possible after the invention of efficient lightweight motors, nearly four centuries after Leonardo's death.

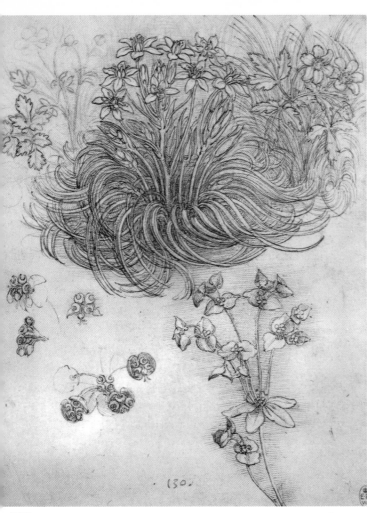

Leonardo used his skill as a great draughtsman to record the complex details of plant forms. His delicate use of shading makes the form of the plant quite clear to the viewer. It is not simply a plant drawing, but a work of art.

Study of a Star of Bethlehem, spurge, and other plants, drawn about 1506

PLANT STUDIES

Even in his earliest paintings, Leonardo had shown a keen interest in copying nature precisely. He drew plants throughout his life, and studied their proportions closely. He concluded that the diverse shapes in nature were not random, as they seemed. The shape of a plant, for example, reflected its transformation from a tiny seed to a seedling, and then to a leafy plant many times larger.

DRAWING FROM NATURE

Plants are ideal subjects for drawing practice. They form complex shapes, and have a variety of textures. To draw them accurately, you need patience.

First look at the overall shape of the plant and the proportions of its different parts: leaves, stem and flowers. Study also the spaces between all these elements. Look closely at the plant and try to draw exactly what you see. To make the structure of the plant clear, you may have to use shading.

As Leonardo knew, the process of drawing will give you a much deeper understanding of a plant. By drawing it, you will look at it more closely than you have ever done before, and discover things you have never noticed.

THE BATTLE OF ANGHIARI

In 1503 Leonardo was asked to paint a large mural (wall painting) in the Palazzo Vecchio, the old palace of Florence. What he planned was even more ambitious than "The Last Supper". Another great Renaissance artist, Michelangelo, was asked to work on a similar mural for the same room. Unfortunately, neither artist finished his project.

UNFINISHED MASTERPIECES

Leonardo spent ten months in 1502-3 away from Florence, working for Cesare Borgia, the powerful and ruthless general of the pope's army. Leonardo was commissioned to make surveys of the pope's lands, and travelled around central Italy drawing many maps. He drew precise aerial views of towns and cities, more detailed and accurate than any other maps of the time.

When he returned to Florence, Leonardo began work on the huge mural for the Palazzo Vecchio. The subject was the Battle of Anghiari of 1440, in which the Florentines had won a famous victory over the army of Milan. Michelangelo (1475-1564) was working on the Battle of Cascina, in which Florence defeated Pisa.

Leonardo also began work on a painting entitled *Leda and the Swan*, based on a Greek myth. Drawings show his typically delicate touch. Only copies of the painting by other artists have survived.

Leonardo's *Battle of Anghiari* was an enormous undertaking. The space it was to fill measured 16.7 by 6 metres (55 by 20 feet). The artist made sketches, completed the cartoon and the middle section of the painting. These were admired, and became models for numerous later battle scenes, but only the sketches have survived.

 Studies for the head of *Leda*, drawn in about 1508

A study of horses for *The Battle of Anghiari*, sketched in about 1504

Leonardo believed that human beings and animals had many similarities in terms of anatomy and emotion. He wanted the taut muscles and bared teeth of the horses here to express fear and fury.

THE HEAT OF BATTLE

Leonardo's sketches for *The Battle of Anghiari* express great ferocity. His drawings show warriors clashing over a tangle of wheeling horses in the heat of battle. He based much of the detail of the painting on historical accounts of the battle.

As usual, Leonardo was not content to paint this vast mural by tried-and-tested methods. He used oil-based colours on polished plaster. This decision soon presented him with frustrating technical problems. The paint would not dry and began to run, possibly because it would not stick properly to the plaster. In the end Leonardo simply abandoned the project.

A sketch for the central section of *The Battle of Anghiari*, drawn in 1503

MAKING SKETCHES

Artists often make sketches of a subject before they begin work on a painting. Sketches help the artist to become familiar with the subject and to decide which composition works best.

Below is a coloured sketch, done on the spot for the watercolour at the top of page 18. The artist hasn't bothered to fill in details that repeat themselves. But she has drawn features such as the windows in great detail, so that she has more information to help her back at the studio. Get into the habit of carrying a sketch book around with you, to jot down ideas and things you see that interest you, that you may want to work on later.

25 —

RETURN TO MILAN

In 1506 Charles d'Amboise, the French governor in Milan, invited Leonardo to work in Milan again. Leonardo was pleased to accept, and spent the next six years there, broken only by a short stay in Florence in 1507-8. He completed only a few paintings. Most of his time was occupied with scientific study, including anatomical research at the hospital (shown left).

ARTIST OF ANATOMY

In Milan Leonardo received a generous salary from King Louis XII of France, and was allowed to do more or less what he chose. He gave advice on architecture and on canals. He also continued his research into anatomy, concentrating on the workings of the human heart and development of the unborn child. His anatomical research, and the detailed drawings which he made of his findings, were probably the most advanced of his time. Leonardo wanted to discover precisely how the human body worked – not only its limbs and internal organs, but also its feelings and emotions. He also made studies of optics (the workings of the eye), and of rock formations and plants.

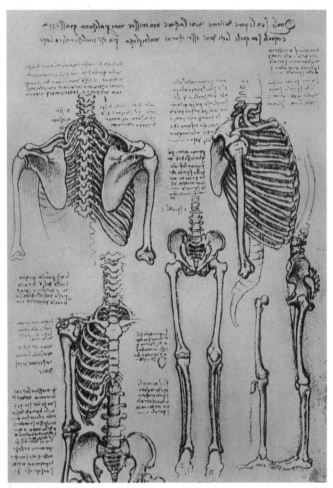

These studies of a human skeleton were drawn in 1510.

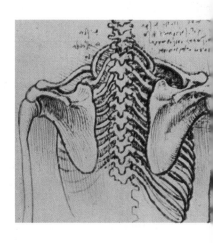

Leonardo's drawings demonstrate the power of illustration to convey knowledge. No one had produced scientific illustrations like these before. The artist used words only to explain what cannot be seen.

Leonardo did little painting in this second Milan period. He took with him sketches and cartoons for a painting, *Virgin and Child with St Anne*, which he completed in about 1510. He may also have finished the second version of *The Virgin of the Rocks* at this time. Like all great artists, Leonardo had students and assistants in his studio. One of these was Francesco Melzi, a faithful pupil who remained with Leonardo until his death.

Leonardo had gained complete mastery in modelling the human face. The Virgin and St Anne in this painting have the same kind of features as the women of Leonardo's early portraits. Their expressions are serene and tender.

Virgin and Child with St Anne, completed about 1510

A CHALLENGING COMPOSITION

Leonardo's painting changed little in 30 years. The painting above has the familiar near-and-far effect. Yet despite this he was still experimenting. The composition of this painting presented a challenge. Mary sits on the knee of her mother, St Anne, and reaches for the child Jesus, who is playing with a lamb. The faces are all in a straight line, but the shoulders of the adults form a triangle which points towards the head of Jesus and the head of the lamb. The composition, however, is not entirely successful. The weight of the Virgin does not seem to rest properly on the lap of her mother.

AERIAL PERSPECTIVE

Leonardo invented the "perspectograph", a tool used by artists to measure "linear" perspective (see page 7). He is also believed to have developed a second kind of perspective, called "aerial perspective". The artist noticed that the colours of hills, buildings and trees change in a measurable way according to how far away they are. Normally they become increasingly light and cool (or bluish) in tone the closer they are to the horizon. This observation has been used by artists ever since to produce the effect of distance. Try painting a landscape yourself. See if painting distant objects bluish gives your work a sense of depth.

FINAL YEARS

In 1513 the French were forced out of Milan, and war again brought change to Leonardo's life. He first went to Rome, where he stayed for three frustrating years as a guest of Giuliano de Medici, brother of the new pope, Leo X. In 1516 he was invited by the French king, Francis I, to live in France, near his summer palace (shown left). He gladly accepted.

ROME AND FRANCE

Leonardo travelled to Rome with his assistants. Rome was going through an exciting transformation, and the artists Michelangelo and Raphael were both there. But Leonardo was now over 60 years old; he was tired, and felt unappreciated in Rome. He had rooms in the Vatican, and continued his studies in optics, mirrors, mechanics and geometry.

In 1516 he accepted an offer from King Francis I of France to stay near the palace of Cloux at Amboise on the River Loire. Leonardo spent most of his time there arranging his papers. He died at Amboise in 1519 at the age of 67.

Self-portrait by Leonardo, aged about 60, drawn in 1512

Leonardo's self-portrait is a remarkably powerful drawing. The lines are fluid, and the shading is carefully controlled. Yet the portrait has a brooding intensity about it. It suggests an inner energy and perhaps a certain frustration. Here is a man who had worked with great energy all his life, yet felt so much remained undone.

Leonardo's *St John the Baptist* is strange and haunting picture. The face is rather feminine, a little like *The Mona Lisa*. The picture is painted in shades of one colour against a dark background. St John's gesture of pointing echoes that of the angel in *The Virgin of the Rocks*.

St John the Baptist, begun in about 1509 and completed about 1515

FINAL WORKS

As before, in Rome and France Leonardo did little painting. He was criticised for this, because many people believed that he had wasted his talents as a painter in favour of his scientific studies, which they did not understand.

In France he planned a palace and garden for King Francis I, and designed some court festivals. He also worked on some dramatic drawings of floods, illustrating the great power of nature. The only painting which he completed during this period was his *St John the Baptist*, which he had begun in Milan.

Leonardo was exceptional in being a great inventor and a very accomplished draughts-man, so he could develop his ideas on paper with amazing skill. The giant crossbow he designed, shown here, would have been over 26 metres long. But anyone can try their hand at inventions. Try to dream up a device that would help you or someone you know. Make quick sketches first to sort out any problems, then a more detailed drawing.

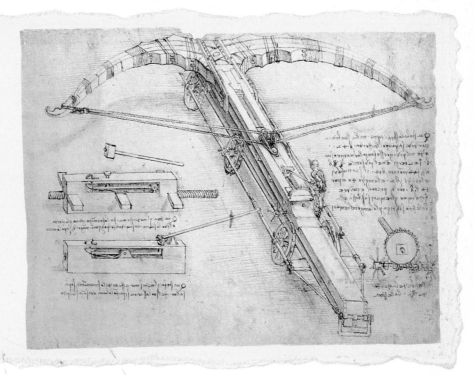

Chronology of Da Vinci's Life

1452 Born near Vinci, in Tuscany, Italy.

1467 Joined the studio of Andrea del Verrocchio in Florence at the start of a six-year apprenticeship.

1472 Became a member of the Guild of St Luke, a painters' guild in Florence.

1473 Painted *The Annunciation*.

1477 (-81) Worked as an independent artist at his own studio in Florence.

1481 Painted *The Adoration of the Magi*

1482 (-99) Went to work in Milan at the invitation of Duke Ludovico Sforza

1483-5 Painted the first version of *The Virgin of the Rocks*.

1493 Clay model for the statue of Francesco Sforza put on display.

1495-8 Painted *The Last Supper*

1500 Went to Mantua after Milan was captured by French troops. From there he went to Venice and Florence.

1502 Worked for 10 months as military architect and surveyor for Cesare Borgia in central Italy.

1503 (-06) Back in Florence. Painted *The Mona Lisa* and started work on *The Battle of Anghiari* (unfinished).

1506 (-13) Returned to Milan at the invitation of Charles d'Amboise.

1510 Completed *Virgin and Child with St Anne*.

1513 (-16) Went to Rome at the invitation of Guiliano de Medici.

1516 (-19) Went to Amboise on the River Loire at the invitation of King Francis 1 of France.

1519 Died at Amboise, aged 67

A Brief History of Art

The world's earliest works of art are figurines dating from 30,000 BC. Cave art developed from 16,000 BC. In the Classical Age (500-400 BC) sculpture flourished in Ancient Greece.

The Renaissance period began in Italy in the 1300s and reached its height in the 16th century. Famous Italian artists include Giotto (c1266-1337), **Leonardo da Vinci** (1452-1519), Michelangelo Buonarroti (1475-1564) and Titian (c1487-1576).

In Europe during the 15th and 16th centuries Hieronymus Bosch (active 1480-1516), Albrecht Dürer (1471-1528), Pieter Breughel the Elder (1525-69) and El Greco (1541-1614) produced great art. Artists of the Baroque period include Peter Paul Rubens (1577-1640) and Rembrandt van Rijn (1606-69).

During the Romantic movement English artists JMW Turner (1775-1851) and John Constable (1776-1837) produced wonderful landscapes. Francisco Goya (1746-1828) was a great Spanish portrait artist.

Impressionism began in France in the 1870s. Artists include Claude Monet (1840-1926), Camille Pissarro (1830-1903) and Edgar Degas (1834-1917). Post-impressionists include Paul Cézanne (1839-1906), Paul Gauguin (1848-1903) and Vincent Van Gogh (1853-90).

The 20th century has seen many movements in art. Piet Mondrian (1872-1944) painted in the Cubist tradition, Salvador Dali (1904-89) in the Surrealist. Pablo Picasso (1881-1973) was a prolific Spanish painter. More recently Jackson Pollock (1912-56) and David Hockney (1937-) have achieved fame.

Museums & galleries

The museums and galleries listed below have examples of Leonardo da Vinci's work:

The Uffizi Gallery, Florence, Italy

Ambrosiana Library, Milan, Italy

Santa Maria delle Grazie, Milan, Italy

The Louvre, Paris, France

Bibliothèque de l'Institut de France, Paris

The National Gallery, London, England

Metropolitan Museum of Art, New York

The National Gallery, Washington DC, USA

The Hermitage, St Petersberg, Russia

Czartoryski Gallery, Cracow, Poland

Alte Pinakothek, Munich, Germany

Biblioteca Nacional, Madrid

British Museum, London, England

The Royal Library, Windsor, England

INDEX

INDEX OF PICTURES

Special thanks to: The Royal Collection © Her Majesty Queen Elizabeth II. Bridgeman Art Library. Biblioteca Reale, Turin. Czartoryski Museum, Cracow. Richard McLanathan.
The publishers have made every effort to contact all the relevant copyright holders and apologise for any omissions that may have inadvertently been made.